SPOTLIGHT ON SPACE SCIENCE

JOURNEY TO VENUS

J.M. SNYDER

PowerKids
press.

New York

Published in 2015 by The Rosen Publishing Group, Inc.
29 East 21st Street, New York, NY 10010

First Edition

Editor: Susan Meyer
Book Design: Kris Everson

Photo Credits: Cover (main), p. 13 (Venus) NASA/JPL; cover (small Venus image), pp. 13 (Earth), 17, 25, 27 NASA; p. 5 Brocken Inaglory; p. 7 Mopic/Shutterstock.com; p. 9 WP; p. 11 NASA/SDO, AIA; p. 15 NASA/JPL/USGS; pp. 19, 29 ESA; p. 21 NASA Planetary Photojournal; p. 23 NASA/JPL/ESA.

Library of Congress Cataloging-in-Publication Data

Snyder, J.M.
Journey to Venus / by J.M. Snyder.
p. cm. — (Spotlight on space science)
Includes index.
ISBN 978-1-4994-0380-0 (pbk.)
ISBN 978-1-4994-0409-8 (6-pack)
ISBN 978-1-4994-0436-4 (library binding)
1.Venus (Planet) — Juvenile literature. 2. Venus (Planet) — Exploration — Juvenile literature. I. Snyder, J.M. II. Title.
QB621.S693 2015
523.42—d23

Manufactured in the United States of America

CPSIA Compliance Information: Batch #CW15PK: For Further Information contact Rosen Publishing, New York, New York at 1-800-237-9932

CONTENTS

EARTH'S TWIN?

CHAPTER 1

Look into the dark sky on a clear night, and you will see a bright object that could be mistaken for a star. The shining, starlike object is actually a planet. It is Venus, our nearest planetary neighbor.

From Earth, Venus is the brightest planet in the solar system. It looks so bright to us because it is covered with yellowish-white clouds that reflect the Sun's light.

Venus formed at the same time and in the same way as Earth. It is nearly the same size as our planet and has a similar **mass**. Venus, however, is a very different world from our own.

If you could stand on Venus, the surface pressure would make it feel as if you were standing 0.5 mile (0.8 km) under the ocean. In fact, the pressure is so great that you would be crushed instantly.

Venus can be seen from Earth with the naked eye. It looks like a very bright star because it reflects the light from the Sun.

That would be, of course, if you hadn't already been burned to a crisp by temperatures that are hot enough to melt lead!

THE FORMATION OF THE SOLAR SYSTEM

CHAPTER 2

Venus, Earth, and the other planets in the solar system were created when our Sun formed about 4.5 billion years ago.

Before the solar system came into being, there was a huge cloud of gas and dust in space. Over time, the cloud collapsed on itself. Most of the gas and dust formed a massive spinning sphere, or ball. As the sphere spun in space, a disk formed around the sphere from the remaining gas and dust.

As all this matter rotated, the sphere pulled in more gas and dust, adding to its size, weight, and **gravity**. The weight of all the material pressing onto the center of the sphere caused the center to get hotter and hotter. Finally, the temperature inside the sphere got so hot that the sphere ignited to become a new star. This new star was our Sun!

The solar system was once a mass of spinning dust and gas.

Inside the rotating disk, other masses formed. These became the solar system's planets, their moons, and smaller objects such as asteroids, **meteoroids**, and **comets**.

THE PLANETS OF THE SOLAR SYSTEM

CHAPTER 3

For around 4.5 billion years, the planets in our solar system have been orbiting the Sun, each taking its own path, or orbit, around our star.

Earth, the third planet from the Sun, takes 365 days to make one orbit. The more distant planets, however, take much longer. For example, Neptune makes one full orbit every 60,190 Earth days!

Five of the solar system's planets—Mercury, Venus, Mars, Jupiter, and Saturn—were known about from earliest times. Then, in March 1781, the British astronomer Sir William Herschel observed Uranus for the first time. At first, he thought he'd seen a comet.

In September 1846, German astronomer Johann Gottfried Galle discovered Neptune, and in 1930, American astronomer Clyde Tombaugh discovered tiny, distant Pluto.

Venus is Earth's closest planetary neighbor in space.

For decades, our solar system was home to nine planets. Then, in 2006, the International Astronomical Union reclassified Pluto as a **dwarf planet** because of its small size. Also, it does not have the gravitational power to pull all the objects close to it into its orbit like the other "true" planets.

TRANSITS OF VENUS

CHAPTER 4

One of the ways that Venus can be seen from Earth is when it passes between Earth and the Sun. When this happens, Venus can be seen as a tiny black dot passing across the face of the Sun. This is called a transit.

Transits of Venus follow a predictable pattern. A transit will occur. Then, eight years later, it will happen again. Then, 121.5 years will pass. Then two transits, separated by eight years, will again take place. Then, 105.5 years will pass before the next pair of transits, again separated by eight years. Then another 121.5 years must pass before the next transit, and so on and so on! The last transit of Venus happened in June 2012. Now, the world will not see this event again until the years 2117 and 2125.

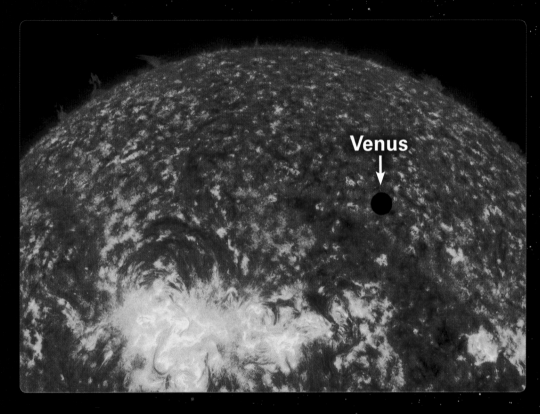

Venus

Venus's transit across the Sun is sometimes visible from Earth. This happened in 2012 and will next occur in 2117.

In 1639, British astronomer Jeremiah Horrocks was the first person to view a transit of Venus. Horrocks directed an image of the Sun through his telescope onto a piece of paper so he could safely watch the transit without looking right at the Sun.

LONG DAYS AND SHORT YEARS

CHAPTER 5

A year, or the time it takes Earth to make one full orbit of the Sun, lasts for 365 days. As Earth orbits, it also rotates, or turns, on its axis, making one full rotation every 24 hours. This is the time period that we call a day. Like Earth, Venus also has years and days.

To orbit the Sun, Earth makes a journey of nearly 560 million miles (901 million km). Venus is closer to the Sun, however, so its journey is shorter at just over 421 million miles (678 million km). This means that Venus can make one orbit of the Sun every 225 Earth days. So a year on Venus is 140 days shorter than on Earth.

Venus, however, rotates on its axis much slower than Earth. It takes 243 Earth days for Venus to make one full rotation.

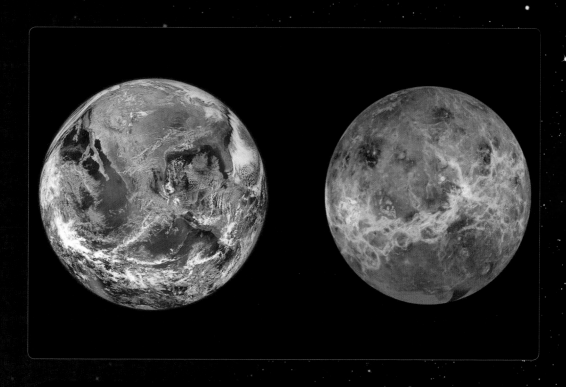

Earth and Venus are very similar in size, but very different in appearance. Venus's thick atmosphere makes it far too hot to support life.

PEELING BACK THE LAYERS
CHAPTER 6

The diameter of Venus is 7,521 miles (12,104 km) across. That's just 398 miles (641 km) smaller than the diameter of Earth.

Scientists think the interior of Venus is very similar to the layers of metal and rock that make up the inside of our planet. At the very center of Venus is a core of iron. Surrounding the core is a layer called the mantle, which is about 1,800 miles (2,897 km) thick. Like Earth's mantle, this layer of Venus is made up of rock and **molten** rock.

The outer layer of the planet is a crust of rock that, in places, is 19 miles (31 km) deep.

Venus has slightly less mass than Earth, so the surface gravity on Venus is about 91 percent of the gravity on Earth. This means that if you weigh 100 pounds (45 kg) on Earth, you would weigh 91 pounds (41 kg) on Venus.

False color was added to this composite photo of Venus to show the varieties of elevation on the planet.

A STIFLING ATMOSPHERE
CHAPTER 7

Like its neighbor Earth, Venus is surrounded by a thick atmosphere made of gases.

Earth's atmosphere contains a mixture of gases, including oxygen, that makes it possible for living things to breathe and survive on Earth. Venus's atmosphere is very different. It is made mostly of **carbon dioxide gas** with just a small quantity of nitrogen and traces of water vapor.

Above the dense layer of gases are thick clouds formed from **sulfur dioxide gas** and droplets of **sulfuric acid**. Venus's top layer of clouds hurtles around the planet driven by winds that travel at 220 miles per hour (354 km/hr). These winds are far faster and stronger than most hurricane-force winds here on Earth! It is these clouds that give Venus a yellowish color. Bursts of lightning have also been detected coming from Venus's acid

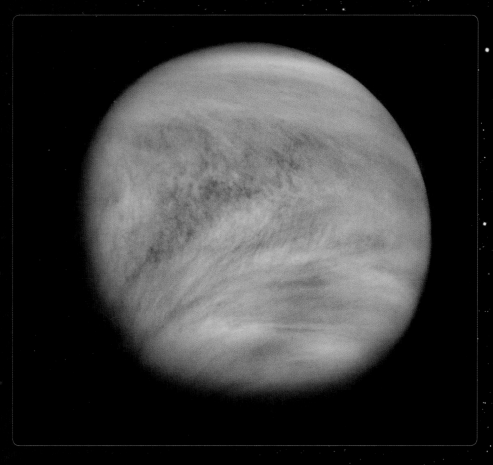

This photo of Venus's thick atmosphere was taken by the Hubble Space Telescope. It used ultraviolet wavelengths to capture the patterns of the clouds.

clouds. Closer to the planet's surface, the winds are far less fierce, traveling at just a few miles (km) per hour.

THE HOTTEST PLANET
CHAPTER 8

Venus is not the nearest planet to the Sun, but it is the hottest planet in the solar system. This is because of an effect that we also experience here on Earth called the greenhouse effect.

For decades, people on Earth have been burning fuels such as coal and oil. Burning these fuels releases gases such as carbon dioxide, methane, and nitrous oxide into Earth's atmosphere. These gases build up in the atmosphere and trap the Sun's heat on Earth, just as heat gets trapped in a greenhouse. On Earth, the greenhouse effect is causing temperatures to rise and **climate change** to happen. The greenhouse effect happens naturally on Earth, but human activities have added to it.

On Venus, the planet's naturally occurring carbon dioxide atmosphere also causes a greenhouse effect. Venus's atmosphere only allows about

Scientists believe that the sulfuric acid in Venus's atmosphere could be electrically charged. This would lead to lightning on the planet's surface.

10 percent of the Sun's heat through to the planet's surface. Once that heat is there, however, it is trapped by the thick blanket of carbon dioxide. This extreme greenhouse effect means that day or night, the temperature on the surface of Venus is a scorching 860°F (460°C)!

UNCOVERING VENUS'S LANDSCAPE

CHAPTER 9

Venus's thick covering of clouds makes it impossible to see the planet's surface with telescopes and equipment that use light waves. **Radar**, however, can penetrate the clouds and uses radio waves to "see" and create images.

Radar equipment sends out radio waves that bounce off an object, such as the surface of Venus. By analyzing the length of time it takes the wave to return and the length of the wave, radar equipment on Earth and aboard spacecraft that have visited the planet can create three-dimensional images. These images have been used to map Venus and reveal to us the planet's fascinating surface.

Images of Venus show a landscape of rolling plains, huge impact craters, mountains, and more than 1,000 volcanoes. Much of the planet's surface is

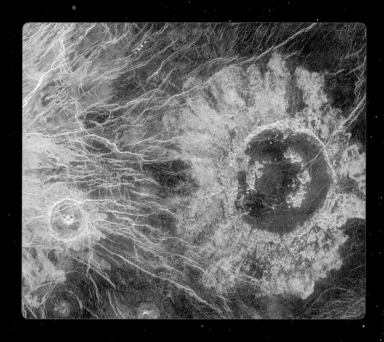

This image of Wheatley Crater was created by Magellan using radar. The crater is 46 miles (74 km) wide.

covered with basalt rock. This rock forms when melted rock from inside a planet erupts onto the surface as lava and then cools and hardens. Lava on Venus erupted from volcanoes and cracks in the planet's crust.

MAPPING VENUS'S LANDMARKS

CHAPTER 10

Radar mapping of Venus has shown that the planet has two vast highland areas. One of these areas, named Ishtar Terra, is near the planet's north pole.

Ishtar Terra is an area larger than Australia. It is home to volcanoes and the planet's four main mountain ranges. Venus's tallest mountain, Maxwell Montes, is also in Ishtar Terra. Maxwell Montes is 7 miles (11 km) tall. That's about 1.5 miles (2.4 km) taller than Mount Everest, the tallest mountain on Earth.

Ishtar Terra is also home to many volcanoes. Some of the area's volcanoes are named for famous women from history, including Sacagawea and Cleopatra.

Venus has a history of volcanic eruptions, and it has been resurfaced many times by fresh lava flows over the billions of years of its lifetime.

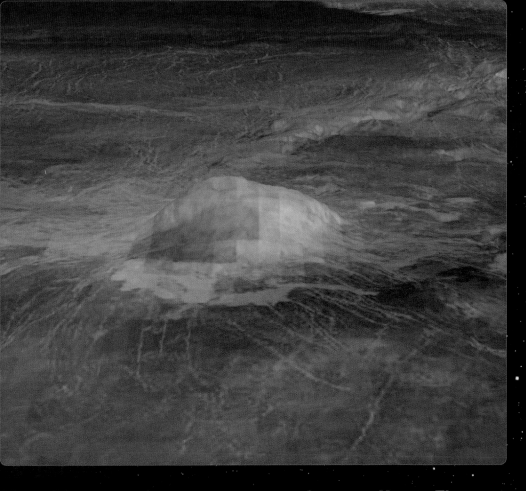

Idunn Mons, seen here, is an active volcano on Venus. The color in this image was added to show the variation in heat.

MARINER 2 AND THE VENERA PROGRAM

CHAPTER 11

In 1962, NASA's *Mariner 2* became the first spacecraft to reach another planet and then send data back to Earth. Since *Mariner 2's* mission to Venus, many spacecraft have orbited and even landed on the planet.

From the early 1960s to early 1980s, the Soviet Union's Venera space program sent a series of spacecraft to Venus. The Venera program claimed many firsts for space exploration, and ten of the *Venera* spacecraft even landed on the planet's surface.

In 1967, *Venera 4* became the first spacecraft to enter the atmosphere of another planet. Then, in 1970, *Venera 7* was the first spacecraft to make a soft landing on another planet. In 1975, *Venera 9* was

This photo of Venus was taken by Mariner 2 *back in 1974.*

the first spacecraft to send pictures from another planet's surface back to Earth.

The spacecraft that landed on Venus did not survive for long before being destroyed by the heat and crushing surface pressure. *Venera 12*, which was sent to study Venus's atmosphere, survived the longest. It landed and then stayed in touch with Earth for 110 minutes.

A ROBOTIC EXPLORER

On May 4, 1989, the **space shuttle** *Atlantis* blasted off from Earth. Aboard was a robotic spacecraft named *Magellan*.

The following day, *Magellan* became the first spacecraft to be launched into space from a space shuttle. Fifteen months later, in August 1990, *Magellan* reached its destination and went into orbit around Venus.

Magellan's mission was to bounce radio waves off the planet's surface and transmit the results back to Earth. Images captured by *Magellan* showed surface winds, craters, and volcanoes. Its imagery showed that about 85 percent of Venus's surface is covered with ancient lava flows. Using radar, *Magellan* was able to create images of 98 percent of Venus's surface.

On October 12, 1994, the control crew on Earth gave *Magellan* its final command. It was to plunge

Magellan *observed Venus from 1990 to 1994. Its mission was divided into 243-day cycles. This is the amount of time it took Venus to rotate once under Magellan's orbit.*

into Venus's atmosphere. *Magellan* carried out its final task, transmitting data until it burned up. Its highly successful mission was over.

VENUS EXPRESS

CHAPTER 13

On November 9, 2005, the European Space Agency launched the *Venus Express* spacecraft. After a five-month-long journey through space, *Venus Express* went into orbit around Venus on April 11, 2006.

Venus Express was sent to study the planet's surface, volcanic activity, atmosphere, hurricane-force winds, and extreme greenhouse effect. It was also sent to examine the ways in which Venus and Earth are the same and different. One of its most exciting discoveries has been changes in the amount of sulfur dioxide in the upper atmosphere. Rising and then falling levels of this gas, which is produced by volcanoes, could mean that volcanic eruptions are still taking place on the planet's surface today.

Many spacecraft have visited Venus, but our superhot, mysterious neighbor still has lots of secrets to reveal. One of the biggest questions

Venus Express used Venus's atmosphere to slow down. This technique is called aerobraking.

still to be answered is why a planet similar in size and formed from the same materials as Earth has developed into such a different world from our own over the past 4.5 billion years.

GLOSSARY

carbon dioxide gas: A gas that's produced when people and animals breathe out, which is used by plants for energy.

climate change: Significant change in the measures of climate over a long period of time.

comet: A body in space made up of dust, gas, and ice that orbits the Sun. It sometimes develops a bright, long tail.

dwarf planet: A body in space that orbits the Sun and is shaped like a sphere but is not large enough to disturb other objects from its orbit.

gravity: The attraction of the mass of a body in space for other bodies nearby.

mass: The amount of matter in something.

meteoroid: A piece of rocky or metal-like matter traveling through space.

molten: Turned to liquid by heat.

radar: A device that sends out radio waves for finding the position and speed of a moving object.

space shuttle: A spacecraft that can be used more than once and that carries people into outer space and back to Earth.

sulfur dioxide gas: A colorless, smelly gas formed by burning sulfur.

sulfuric acid: A strong mineral acid that can eat away at certain substances.

FOR MORE INFORMATION

BOOKS

Aguilar, David A. *13 Planets: The Latest View of the Solar System*. Washington, D.C.: National Geographic, 2011.

Hollar, Sherman. *The Inner Planets: Mercury, Venus, and Mars*. New York, NY: Britannica Educational Publishing, 2012.

Taylor-Butler, Christine. *Planet Venus*. New York, NY: Children's Press, 2014.

WEBSITES

Due to the changing nature of Internet links, PowerKids Press has developed an online list of websites related to the subject of this book. This site is updated regularly. Please use this link to access the list: www.powerkidslinks.com/soss/venu

INDEX